T0058549

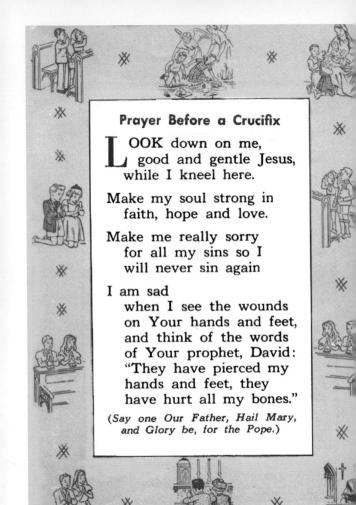

Prayer Before a Crucifix

LOOK down on me,
good and gentle Jesus,
while I kneel here.

Make my soul strong in
faith, hope and love.

Make me really sorry
for all my sins so I
will never sin again

I am sad
when I see the wounds
on Your hands and feet,
and think of the words
of Your prophet, David:
"They have pierced my
hands and feet, they
have hurt all my bones."

*(Say one Our Father, Hail Mary,
and Glory be, for the Pope.)*

This Missal Belongs To

Name ....

School ....

Date ....

*   *   *

I received My

FIRST HOLY COMMUNION

on.................................. .... at the Church

of ....

Pastor ....

*   *   *

I received the Sacrament of

CONFIRMATION

on.......................... .... at the Church

of ....

Bishop ....

Sponsor ....

Latin Mass

CHILDREN'S MISSAL

At Mass Jesus Comes to Save Us

Latin Mass

CHILDREN'S MISSAL

An Easy Way of

PRAYING THE MASS

for Boys and Girls

By

REV. H. HOEVER, S.O.Cist., Ph.D.

De Permissu Superiorum

Nihil Obstat:

> JOHN A. GOODWINE, J.C.D.
> > *Censor Librorum*

Imprimatur:

> ✠ FRANCIS CARDINAL SPELLMAN
> > *Archbishop of New York*

January 3, 1959

> All the First Degree responses for a Dialogue Mass as indicated by the Instruction of the Sacred Congregation of Rites, dated September 3, 1958, are included in their proper place. In addition, the complete Latin text of the *Our Father* has been provided.

ISBN: 978-1-930873-17-9

Printed and bound in India.

Neumann Press
Charlotte, North Carolina
www.NeumannPress.com

2013

CONTENTS

Grateful acknowledgment is made to Rev. Mother Kathryn Sullivan, R.S.C.J., of Manhattanville College of the Sacred Heart, Purchase, N. Y., for her painstaking and scholarly suggestions in editing this book.

Dear Boys and Girls:

THIS is your own missal. Take it with you when you go to Mass. It will help you to please God, to adore and thank Him, to praise and love Him.

On every page you will find a picture and a prayer. The picture will show you what the priest is doing. The prayer will help you to pray with the priest.

Every Sunday the priest reads a gospel that will teach you something that Jesus said or did. Study the picture and read the gospel story before you come to church. During the day think about what you have read and talk to Jesus about it. In this way you will grow more and more like Him.

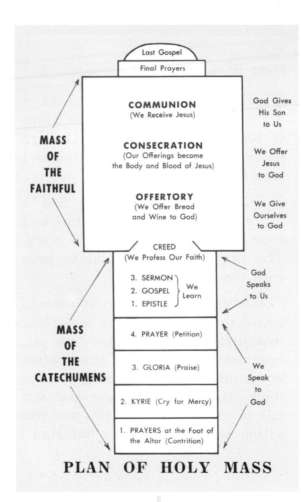

Last Gospel

Final Prayers

COMMUNION
(We Receive Jesus)

God Gives
His Son
to Us

MASS OF THE FAITHFUL

CONSECRATION
(Our Offerings become
the Body and Blood of Jesus)

We Offer
Jesus
to God

OFFERTORY
(We Offer Bread
and Wine to God)

We Give
Ourselves
to God

CREED
(We Profess Our Faith)

3. SERMON
2. GOSPEL   } We Learn
1. EPISTLE

God
Speaks
to Us

MASS OF THE CATECHUMENS

4. PRAYER (Petition)

3. GLORIA (Praise)

2. KYRIE (Cry for Mercy)

1. PRAYERS at the Foot of
the Altar (Contrition)

We
Speak
to
God

PLAN OF HOLY MASS

HOLY MASS

ON Calvary Christ offered His Body and Blood to God the Father for us. In the Mass this great act is repeated.

Every Mass has two parts:
1. The Mass of the Catechumens.
2. The Mass of the Faithful.

During the *Mass of the Catechumens,* we speak to God in acts of contrition (when the priest prays at the foot of the altar), in acts of desire, of praise, of petition (when the priest says the Kyrie, the Gloria, the Prayers). Then we listen to what God says to us in the Epistle, the Gospel, and the Sermon.

The *Mass of the Faithful* begins with the Creed. Then, with the priest, we offer the bread and wine which is changed at the Consecration into the Body and Blood of Christ. In Holy Communion we receive Christ whom we love.

The SACRIFICE of CALVARY is Renewed in the Mass

On Calvary Jesus offered Himself as the Sacrificial Gift.

On Calvary the One who sacrificed His life was Jesus, without any ministers.

On Calvary Jesus merited graces for us.

On Calvary Jesus really suffered and died.

At Every Mass I Should —

1. Remember that our Lord wants me to assist at Holy Mass on Sundays and Holy Days of obligation.

2. Remember that our Lord is very pleased when I come to Holy Mass on week days.

3. Remember to pray for the living and the dead for whom the Mass is being offered.

4. Remember to pray with the priest by using this missal, and to receive Holy Communion.

The SACRIFICE of the MASS is the Same as the Sacrifice of Calvary

In the Mass Jesus offers Himself as the Sacrificial Gift in an unbloody manner.

In the Mass Jesus Himself offers the Holy Sacrifice; the priest is His representative.

In the Mass the merits of Jesus are applied to us.

In the Mass Jesus does not suffer nor die.

At Every Mass I Should —

1. ADORE and THANK God for His great love for me.

2. HONOR and PRAISE God.

3. GIVE myself to God in union with the offering made by Jesus Christ, His Son.

4. ASK God to forgive my sins and to increase my love for Him.

PRAYER BEFORE MASS

I bless myself saying: KNEEL

IN THE Name of the Father, ✠ and of the Son, and of the Holy Ghost. Amen.

O MY Jesus, You came on earth to save the world by dying for us on the cross. You come again in every Mass to show us Your love.

During this Mass I want to thank You for dying for us on the cross and to adore You present on this altar.

Teach me how to become like You.

Bless all whom I love and all for whom I ought to pray.

THE BEGINNING OF HOLY MASS

———

KNEEL

The priest makes the sign of the cross while standing at the foot of the altar. We, too, make the sign of the cross, saying:

IN THE Name of the Father, ✠ and of the Son, and of the Holy Ghost. Amen.

DEAR God, I have come to Mass to adore You, and to thank You for all Your blessings.

I ask You to give Your grace to me and to the whole world.

THE CONFITEOR
We Are Sorry For Our Sins

While the priest bows low to say the Confiteor, we tell God how sorry we are that we have displeased Him.　*KNEEL*

I CONFESS to almighty God, to the blessed Virgin Mary, and to all the saints and angels, that I have sinned.

I hope that almighty God will have mercy on me, forgive me my sins, and lead me to everlasting life. Amen.

May the almighty and merciful Lord take away all my sins and help me come closer to Him. Amen.

THE INTROIT

We Praise God

The priest makes the sign of the cross as he begins to read the Introit.

KNEEL

O ETERNAL Father, I offer You this sacrifice of the Body and Blood of Jesus.

I offer it to thank You for Your goodness and to ask pardon for my sins.

I offer it for my parents, my friends, and for everyone. May we all know You and love You.

THE KYRIE

We Ask God's Mercy

With the priest let us ask God to pardon our sins and all the sins of the world.

KNEEL

LORD, have mercy on us.
Lord, have mercy on us.
Lord, have mercy on us.

CHRIST, have mercy on us.
Christ, have mercy on us.
Christ, have mercy on us.

LORD, have mercy on us.
Lord, have mercy on us.
Lord, have mercy on us.

THE GLORIA

We Praise God

The priest stands at the middle of the altar and repeats the words the angels sang when Jesus was born.

KNEEL

GLORY be to God on high, and on earth peace to men of good will.

We praise You, we bless You, we adore You, we thank You.

O Lord, Jesus Christ, You who take away the sins of the world, have mercy on us.

—————— IN A DIALOGUE MASS ——————

After the Gloria:

Priest: Dóminus vobíscum.
(The Lord be with you.)

ALL: Et cum spí-ri-tu tu-o.
(And with your spirit.)

THE PRAYER

We Pray For All the People

The priest returns to the right side of the altar and reads one or more prayers to God in the name of all the people.

KNEEL

ALMIGHTY God, we thank You for our gift of faith in the Blessed Trinity, one God in three Divine Persons.

O Lord, without You we can do nothing. Help us to keep Your commandments so that we may please You in all things.

―――――― IN A DIALOGUE MASS ――――――

At the end of the Prayer:

Priest: Per ómnia sæcula sæculórum.   ALL: A-men.
    (Forever and ever.)   (Amen.)

THE EPISTLE

God Speaks to Us

The priest reads the Epistle, a passage usually taken from the writings of the Apostles, especially St. Paul.

KNEEL

DEAR Jesus, I am glad to learn more about You. I want to remember Your words.

O Jesus, help me to know my catechism, and to understand all that our priests tell us.

I want to be brave like Saint Paul who loved You so much.

――――――― JN A DIALOGUE MASS ―――――――

At the end of the Epistle:

ALL: **De-o grá-ti-as.** (Thanks be to God.)

THE GOSPEL
God Speaks to Us

The priest goes to the left side of the altar to read what Jesus said and did when He was on earth.

STAND

DEAR Jesus, I believe all the wonderful things Your Holy Gospel tells me.

I am always happy when I read or listen to the beautiful stories of Your life on earth.

Here the priest reads the Gospel aloud.

——————— IN A DIALOGUE MASS ———————

Priest: Dóminus vobíscum.
  (The Lord be with you.)
Priest: Sequéntia sancti Evangélii secúndum N.
(Continuation of the holy Gospel according to St. N. . . .)

ALL: Et cum spí-ri-tu tu-o.
  (And with your spirit.)
ALL: Gló-ri-a ti-bi, Dó-mi-ne.
  (Glory be to You, O Lord.)

At the end of the Gospel:
ALL: La-us ti-bi, Chri-ste. (Praise be to You, O Christ.)

——————————— 20 ———————————

THE CREED
We Believe All That God Teaches

The priest recites the Nicene Creed and we make an act of faith.

STAND

O GOD the Father, I believe that You made the world.

I believe that Jesus Christ is really God and Man, and that He died on the cross for me.

I believe that the Holy Ghost is the third Person of the Blessed Trinity.

——————— IN A DIALOGUE MASS ———————

After the Creed:

Priest: Dóminus vobíscum.
(The Lord be with you.)

ALL: Et cum spí-ri-tu tu-o.
(And with your spirit.)

THE OFFERTORY
We Offer the Bread to God

The priest offers bread to God. Soon it will be changed into the Body of Jesus.

SIT

ALMIGHTY and everlasting God, please accept this spotless host. We offer it to You in sorrow for all the times we have hurt You.

We offer this host for all good people, both living and dead, and we ask You to give them the grace of everlasting life with You.

THE OFFERTORY

The Wine and Water

The priest pours wine and a little water into the chalice.

SIT

O GOD, through the mystery of this wine and water, may we share in Your divine life.

We offer You this chalice of salvation that it may please You and bring salvation to the whole world. We offer You all that we have and all that we are. Please accept our offering.

THE OFFERTORY

We offer the Wine to God

The priest offers the wine to God. Soon it will be changed into the Precious Blood of Jesus.

SIT

O JESUS, You gave Yourself for us on the cross, and You give Yourself again in this Holy Sacrifice of the Mass. I want to give myself to You.

We offer this Mass with the priest for Your glory, and for Your Church.

Please hear our prayers.

WASHING OF HANDS

We Ask God to Purify Our Souls

The priest washes his hands, and prays to God to make him clean in soul and body.

SIT

DEAR God, make our hearts and minds clean.

Take away all sin from our souls so that we may be more pleasing to You.

Help us to think about You more often, and to serve You more obediently. May we be more attentive when we pray, and more kind to others.

THE SECRET

We Speak to God of Our Gifts

The priest reads a prayer called the Secret because it is always read silently.   *SIT*

GRACIOUSLY accept our gifts to You, O Lord, our God, and let them be always a help to us and to all people.

We beg You, almighty God, to bless this offering and to give us the grace to save our souls, through Jesus Christ, our Lord.

——————— IN A DIALOGUE MASS ———————

At the end of the Secret:

Priest: Per ómnia sǽcula sæculórum.
    (Forever and ever.)

ALL: **A-men.**
    (Amen.)

Priest: Dóminus vobíscum.
    (The Lord be with you.)

ALL: **Et cum spí-ri-tu tu-o.**
    (And with your spirit.)

Priest: Sursum corda.
    (Lift up your hearts.)

ALL: **Ha-bé-mus ad Dó-mi-num.**
    (We lift them up to the Lord.)

Priest: Grátias agámus
    Dómino Deo nostro.
(Let us thank the Lord our God.)

ALL: **Dig-num et ju-stum est.**
    (It is fitting and just.)

——————— 26 ———————

THE PREFACE

Our Prayer of Praise and Thanksgiving

The priest recites a prayer of praise and thanksgiving to God.

SIT

WE GIVE thanks to You, O Lord, Father almighty and everlasting God.

Glory be to the Father, and to the Son, and to the Holy Ghost, now and forever. Amen.

The bell rings 3 times:

KNEEL

Holy, Holy, Holy, Lord God of all! Heaven and earth are full of Your glory.

We Pray for the Church

The great moment is fast approaching when our Lord Jesus Christ will come down upon the altar.

KNEEL

O ETERNAL Father, we want to offer ourselves to You with Your Son, our loving Savior, Jesus Christ.

With Him and through Him, we ask You to take care of the Catholic Church all over the world. Keep her in peace, unity, holiness and truth.

We Pray for the Living

We join with the priest in praying for our
dear ones, our relatives and friends.

KNEEL

REMEMBER, O Lord, my
parents, relatives and
friends, for whom we offer this
sacrifice of praise, or who offer
it for themselves, or for their
families and friends.

May this holy sacrifice gain
for them health and salvation,
who offer their praise to You,
eternal, living and true God.

May this offering bring us
peace, and may we one day be
with the saints in heaven.

We Pray to All the Saints in Heaven

Pray with the priest to our Blessed Mother Mary and the saints. They can help us to love God on earth and to be happy with Him in heaven.

KNEEL

O LORD, we remember with love the Blessed Virgin Mary, Your holy apostles and martyrs, and all Your saints. We unite ourselves with them as we offer You this sacrifice.

May the merits and prayers of our Lady and all the saints help us at all times.

Blessed Virgin and all you saints, pray for us at this Holy Mass.

We Ask God to Accept and Bless the Offering of Bread and Wine

When the priest spreads his hands over the chalice, the bell rings once.

BLESS this offering, O Lord, and make it worthy of You. Give us a peaceful life on earth and bring us all safely to You in heaven.

May this offering of bread and wine become the Body and Blood of Jesus.

He died for us on the cross and now in the Holy Sacrifice He comes to us to carry on His work of love.

Elevation of the Sacred Host

Consecration of the Bread

At the Last Supper, on the day before Jesus died on the cross, He took bread into His holy hands. He raised His eyes to You, O God, His almighty Father, and gave thanks to You. He blessed it, broke it and gave it to His disciples, saying: All of you take and eat of this:

FOR THIS IS MY BODY.

While the priest adores the Sacred Host, the bell rings three times. When he elevates the Sacred Host, look at It and say:

MY LORD AND MY GOD!

Consecration of the Wine

The priest bends over and changes the wine into the living Blood of Jesus. He uses the same words which Jesus used at the Last Supper.

KNEEL

For This Is the Chalice of My Blood of the New and Eternal Testament: the Mystery of Faith: Which Shall Be Shed for You, and for Many unto the Forgiveness of Sins.

While the priest adores the Precious Blood in the chalice, the bell rings three times. When he elevates the chalice, look at It and say:

MY JESUS, MERCY!

Elevation of the Precious Blood

We Offer the Victim to God

The priest now recites three short prayers and offers the Body and Blood of Jesus.

KNEEL

WE remember, O Lord, the sufferings of Jesus Christ, our Savior and our Redeemer, who rose victoriously from the dead and ascended gloriously into heaven.

Grant that our sacrifice will be pleasing to You, like the offerings of Abel, Abraham and Melchisedech.

May Your angel bring these offerings to Your heavenly altar so that we may be filled with heavenly blessings.

We Pray for the Dead

With the priest, we remember the souls of all the faithful departed.

KNEEL

REMEMBER, O Lord, the souls of all the faithful who have died, especially those of my friends and relatives.

Through the graces of this Holy Mass, may we all come to eternal life.

May their souls and all the souls of the faithful departed, through the mercy of God, rest in peace. Amen.

The Minor Elevation

We Adore God

The priest makes the sign of the cross with the Host five times over the chalice. Then he elevates both slightly.

KNEEL

O LORD, we trust in Your mercy and You give us all good things through Christ.

Through Him, and with Him, and in Him is all honor and glory to You, God, the Father almighty, in the unity of the Holy Ghost, forever and ever Amen.

─────── IN A DIALOGUE MASS ───────

At the end of the Minor Elevation:

Priest: Per ómnia sǽcula sæculórum.   ALL: A-men.
(Forever and ever.)   (Amen.)

The Our Father

Our preparation for very close union with Jesus in Holy Communion begins with the "Our Father," the prayer of Jesus.

KNEEL

OUR Father, who art in heaven, hallowed be Thy name: Thy kingdom come: Thy will be done on earth as it is in heaven.

Give us this day our daily bread; and forgive us our trespasses, as we forgive those who trespass against us. And lead us not into temptation, but deliver us from evil. Amen.

─────── IN A DIALOGUE MASS ───────

ALL: Pa-ter no-ster, qui es in cæ-lis: / sanc-ti-fi-cé-tur no-men tu-um. / Ad-vé-ni-at reg-num tu-um. / Fi-at vo-lún-tas tu-a, sic-ut in cæ-lo, et in ter-ra. / Pa-nem no-strum quo-ti-di-á-num da no-bis hó-di-e: / et di-mít-te no-bis dé-bi-ta no-stra, / sic-ut et nos di-mít-ti-mus de-bi-tó-ri-bus no-stris. / Et ne nos in-dú-cas in ten-ta-ti-ó-nem; / sed lí-be-ra nos a ma-lo. / A-men.

or

Priest: Et ne nos indúcas in tentatiónem.
ALL: Sed lí-be-ra nos a ma-lo.

We Pray for Peace

The priest takes the paten between his first and second fingers, and says: KNEEL

FREE us, we beg You, O Lord, from all evils, past, present and future; through the help of the blessed and glorious Mary, Mother of God, together with Your blessed apostles and saints.

In Your goodness, grant us peace and freedom from sin.

May we be safe from all evil through Jesus Christ, Your Son, who lives and reigns with You in the unity of the Holy Ghost.

IN A DIALOGUE MASS

At the end of the Prayer for Peace:

Priest: Per ómnia sǽcula sæculórum.
(Forever and ever.)

ALL: A-men.
(Amen.)

Priest: Pax Dómini sit semper vobíscum.

ALL: Et cum spí-ri-tu tu-o.
(And with your spirit.)

(May the peace of the Lord be always with you.)

We Pray to the Lamb of God

The priest breaks the Host over the chalice, dropping a small particle of the Host in the chalice.

KNEEL

MAY this union of the Body and Blood of our Lord Jesus Christ, help us to life everlasting.

Lamb of God, You who take away the sins of the world, have mercy on us. (2 *times.*)

Lamb of God, You who take away the sins of the world, grant us peace.

We Pray to Receive
A Worthy Communion

We pray for the peace of the Church, a worthy Communion and the blessed fruits of the Holy Sacrifice of the Mass.

KNEEL

O LORD Jesus Christ, grant to Your Church peace and unity according to Your Will.

O Lord, by this Your most Sacred Body and Blood, take away all my sins, and protect me from every evil.

May the reception of Your Body and Blood, O Lord, keep me strong in body and soul.

May I always obey Your commandments, and never lose You by sin.

The Priest Receives Holy Communion

The priest, striking his breast with his right hand, and raising his voice a little, says, and we say with him:

KNEEL

L ORD, I am not worthy that You should come to me. Only say the word, and my soul shall be healed. (3 *times.*)

The priest makes the sign of the cross with the Sacred Host, over the paten, saying:

M AY the Body of our Lord Jesus Christ preserve my soul now and forever. Amen.

The priest receives Holy Communion.

We Receive Holy Communion

When the priest lifts up a Sacred Host and turns toward the people, say 3 times:

KNEEL

L ORD, I am not worthy that You should come to me. Only say the word, and my soul shall be healed.

Descending the steps of the altar to the altar rail, the priest administers Holy Communion, saying to each person:

M AY the Body of our Lord Jesus Christ preserve your soul now and forever. Amen.

Purifying the Sacred Vessels

The priest purifies the chalice with a little wine, saying:

SIT

O LORD, we have received Your Sacrament as our food on earth. Grant that it may keep our hearts pure and strengthen us for eternity.

He purifies his fingers with wine and water.

I HAVE received Your Body and Blood, O Lord Jesus, Son of the Eternal Father.

Grant, O Jesus, that no stain of sin remain in me.

The Postcommunion

Prayer of Thanksgiving

At the right side of the altar the priest reads the Postcommunion. SIT

I ADORE You, my Jesus. I worship You, now present in my heart.

I thank You for coming to me, for I want to know You, love You, and serve You as long as I live.

—————— IN A DIALOGUE MASS ——————

Before the Postcommunion:

Priest: Dóminus vobíscum.
(The Lord be with you.)

ALL: Et cum spí-ri-tu tu-o.
(And with your spirit.)

At the end of the Postcommunion:

Priest: Per ómnia sǽcula sæculórum.
(Forever and ever.)

ALL: A-men.
(Amen.)

Final Prayers

Last Blessing

The priest now goes to the middle of the altar and blesses us in the name of the Most Holy Trinity.

KNEEL

O ALMIGHTY God, please bless me: Father, Son and Holy Ghost.

Bless me in every way and bless all those for whom I want to pray.

IN A DIALOGUE MASS

Before the Last Blessing:

Priest: Dóminus vobíscum.
(The Lord be with you.)

ALL: Et cum spí-ri tu tu-o.
(And with your spirit.)

Priest: Benedicámus Dómino.
(Let us bless the Lord.)

ALL: De-o grá-ti-as.
(Thanks be to God.)

or

Ite, Missa est.
(Go, you are dismissed.)

At the end of the Last Blessing: ALL: A-men.

The Last Gospel

The priest goes to the gospel side of the altar and reads the gospel of St. John, which tells us many beautiful things about Jesus.

STAND

JESUS is true God and true Man. He always was and always will be. All things were made by Him.

Jesus came to show men His glory. We must be like Him, for He was full of grace and truth.

——————— IN A DIALOGUE MASS ———————

At the beginning of the Last Gospel:

Priest: Dóminus vobíscum.
(The Lord be with you.)
Priest: Inítium sancti Evangélii secúndum Joánnem.
(Beginning of the holy Gospel according to St. John.)

ALL: Et cum spí-ri-tu tu-o.
(And with your spirit.)
ALL: Gló-ri-a ti-bi, Dó-mi-ne.
(Glory be to You, O Lord.)

At the end of the Last Gospel:

ALL: De-o grá-ti-as. (Thanks be to God.)

Prayers After Low Mass

These are prayers said for the persecuted Church in Russia.

KNEEL

Hail Mary (*3 times*)

HAIL, Holy Queen, Mother of Mercy, our life, our sweetness, and our hope! To you do we cry, poor banished children of Eve; to you do we send up our sighs, mourning and weeping in this valley of tears. Turn then, most gracious advocate, your eyes of mercy toward us; and after this our exile, show us the blessed fruit of your womb, Jesus. O clement, O loving, O sweet Virgin Mary.

Priest: Pray for us, O holy Mother of God.

All: That we may be made worthy of the promises of Christ.

Let us pray.

O GOD, our refuge and our strength, look down in mercy on Your people who cry to You; and by the intercession of the glorious and Immaculate Virgin Mary, Mother of God, of Saint Joseph her spouse, of Your blessed Apostles Peter and Paul, and of all the saints, in mercy and goodness hear our prayers for the conversion of sinners, and for the liberty and exaltation of our holy mother the Church. Through the same Christ our Lord. Amen.

HOLY Michael, the Archangel, defend us in battle; be our safeguard against the wickedness and snares of the devil. May God rebuke him we humbly pray; and do you, Prince of the heavenly host, by the power of God cast into hell Satan and all the evil spirits, who wander through the world seeking the ruin of souls. Amen.

Priest: Most Sacred Heart of Jesus.

All: Have mercy on us. (*3 times.*)

Gospel Stories
for Sundays and Feastdays

Each year the Missal recalls for us the Life, Death, Resurrection and Ascension of Jesus by the arrangement of the Church Year. Therefore, to grow in knowledge and love of Jesus — *pray the Mass* with your Missal.

Outline of the Church Year

ADVENT — Jesus is near.

CHRISTMAS — Jesus is with us.

EPIPHANY — Jesus shows His glory.

TIME AFTER EPIPHANY — Jesus gives lessons for His Church.

SEPTUAGESIMA — Jesus prepares to suffer for all men.

LENT — Jesus suffers and dies.

EASTER — Jesus triumphs over sin and death.

TIME AFTER EASTER — Jesus instructs His apostles.

ASCENSION — Jesus ascends to His heavenly Father.

PENTECOST — From heaven Jesus sends the Holy Ghost to His disciples.

TIME AFTER PENTECOST — The Holy Ghost carries on the work of Jesus through His Church.

The End of the World

OUR Lord was a great prophet. One day He told His disciples many things that will happen at the end of the world. There will be signs in the sun, moon and stars. The sea will roar. Wicked men will be afraid.

He did not tell the disciples when this will happen. That is God's secret. Even His angels in heaven do not know. But He warned the disciples to watch and pray. We, too, must be ready for our Lord when He comes.

2nd SUNDAY OF ADVENT

Christ's Message to John the Baptist

JOHN the Baptist was in prison because Herod feared him. Rumors of Jesus' miracles came to John so he sent two of his disciples to ask Jesus if He was the Savior.

The disciples watched Jesus preach to the poor, cure the sick, make the blind see and the lame walk. Jesus told them to return to John and tell him all they had seen.

John understood in this way that Jesus was truly the Savior who had come to save all men.

John's Preaching

MANY Jews came along the banks of the Jordan to hear John the Baptist preach. They asked if he was the Savior. He answered that he was not. He told them that the Savior was so holy that he was not worthy to untie even the strap of His sandal.

John warned the people to prepare to welcome the Savior who would soon come to them. He told them to prepare for His coming by doing their duty and being just and good.

4th SUNDAY OF ADVENT

Preparation for the Coming of Christ

JOHN the Baptist lived for many years in the desert. When it was time to prepare for the coming of Christ, he went into the lands near the Jordan River, preaching penance and baptizing the people.

He said to the people: "Make ready the way of the Lord, make straight His paths. Every valley shall be filled, every mountain and hill shall be brought low, and the crooked ways shall be made straight, and the rough ways smooth; and all men shall see the salvation of God."

The Birth of Jesus

CHRISTMAS DAY
The Birth of Jesus

THE Roman Emperor Augustus ordered the people in all the countries under his rule to be counted. Joseph and Mary left their home in Nazareth and traveled to Bethlehem. So many people had come to be registered that there was no room for them in the inn. Outside the town, on the hills, they found a cave. Here Jesus was born. Mary wrapped Him and laid Him in a manger.

Nearby, shepherds were watching their sheep. Suddenly an angel appeared and said: "Do not be afraid, for behold, I bring you good news of great joy, for today in the town of Bethlehem a Savior has been born. You will find the infant Jesus lying in a manger." Many other angels appeared; they praised God saying: "Glory be to God in the highest, and on earth peace among men of good will."

SUNDAY WITHIN OCTAVE
OF CHRISTMAS

Jesus Is Carried to the Temple

WHEN Jesus was forty days old, Joseph and Mary carried Him to the Temple to offer Him to God. They brought with them two turtle doves because the Law required it.

An old man named Simeon knew that Jesus was the Son of God. He held the Child in his arms and praised God for His goodness to men. Simeon told Mary that she would have to suffer many things because she loved Jesus.

THE LORD'S CIRCUMCISION

The Holy Name (January 1)

ON New Year's Day the Church reads the beautiful gospel about the Holy Name of Jesus. When a newborn child was only eight days old, it was the custom to choose his name. Mary and Joseph did not have to wonder about the name they would choose because the angel had already told them this name before He was born. So they called Him Jesus.

This name "Jesus" means that He came to save us from our sins, and to bring us to heaven where we will be happy with Him forever.

THE FEAST OF THE HOLY NAME

The Holy Name of Jesus *(Usually Jan. 2)*

JESUS was given a name that tells us that He came into the world to teach us, and to save us from our sins. Jesus taught us by words and example. When He was a child, He was always obedient and good.

When He was a man, He preached and worked many miracles. One day He told the disciples that His Father will give us anything we ask in His Name. We must bow our heads when we say the Holy Name of Jesus, because Jesus loves us and died on the cross for us.

The Coming of the Wise Men

WHEN Jesus was still a baby, three Wise Men came from a far land to Jerusalem. They told Herod, the ruler, that they had seen a star in the East and they had come to adore the newborn King.

Herod feared that this new King would put him off his throne, so he told the Wise Men to find the new King and report to him. They went to Bethlehem and gave Jesus presents of gold, incense and myrrh. They did not go back to Herod but returned home by another way.

FEAST OF THE HOLY FAMILY

Jesus was Lost for Three Days

WHEN Jesus was twelve years old, He went up to Jerusalem with Mary and Joseph. After the feast, His parents started home and discovered that Jesus was not with them. For three days they looked for Him.

At last they went to the Temple. There they found Jesus surrounded by learned men, listening to them and asking them questions. Mary did not understand that Jesus was doing the work of His heavenly Father, but she was happy because He returned obediently to Nazareth.

The Marriage Feast of Cana

ONE day Mary went to a marriage feast in Cana. Jesus and His disciples were also there. Toward the end of the feast, Mary saw that there was not enough wine, so she told Jesus. She knew that He would never refuse to do anything she wanted.

Jesus ordered the waiters to fill six big water jars with water and to carry the water to the steward. Only then was it known that Jesus had turned that same water into wine.

The Good Centurion

WHEN our Lord was living in Palestine, there were many Roman officers in the land. One of these officers was a Centurion, whose servant boy was sick. He loved this boy, and so he asked Jesus to heal him.

Jesus said: "I will come and heal him." The Centurion answered: "Lord, I am not worthy that You should come under my roof. Say only the word and my servant will be healed." Jesus praised the Centurion's faith and cured the boy.

A Storm at Sea

JESUS had preached to many people that day. He was tired. He asked His disciples to row Him across the lake. Then He fell asleep.

Suddenly, a great storm arose, and the boat seemed to be sinking. The disciples became frightened and wakened Jesus. He stood up and told the winds to be still, and then there was a great calm. The disciples were filled with wonder because Jesus was so powerful that even the wind and the seas obeyed Him.

The Sower and His Seed

JESUS often told the people stories about God's goodness. One of these stories was about a man who planted good seed in his field. He had an enemy who came at night and planted bad seeds among the good.

The servants soon discovered the weeds growing in the wheat field, and they wanted to destroy the weeds. But the master said it was better to wait until the harvest; then he would burn the weeds and store the wheat in the barn.

Parables

PARABLES are stories that Jesus used to tell the people to help them to understand His teaching. One day He wanted them to know about the kingdom of heaven; so He told them it was like a little mustard seed which grows until it is a great tree and many birds can come and live in its branches.

This parable helped the people to understand that the Church would at first be little, but then grow, and one day would have many members.

The Workers in the Vineyard

GOD'S ways are full of mystery. Jesus showed this in a story about the workers in the vineyard.

A man owned a vineyard, and he asked many men to work for him. Some worked all day. Some worked for only an hour. He gave them all the same wages.

Those who had worked all day were displeased, but the owner said he had been fair. God, too, can give a heavenly reward to those who live a short life or a long life.

The Sower and the Seed

NOT all the seed that a farmer plants will grow. The birds eat some of the seeds. Seeds that fall on rocks and stones soon die. But the seed that falls on good ground will grow to a great harvest.

Jesus said that God's word is like these seeds. Some souls soon forget what God wants. Others listen carefully and always do what pleases Him. Jesus praised all who remember His words and try to serve Him. We must pray for missionaries who preach God's word.

Jesus Cures a Blind Man

A BLIND man sat on the roadside. He was waiting for Jesus. When he heard that Jesus was near, he cried: "Jesus, Son of David, have mercy on me." Jesus stopped and asked that the blind man be brought to Him.

When the man came to Jesus, he asked: "Lord, that I may see." Jesus said: "Receive your sight, your faith has saved you." The man could see again, and went away praising the goodness of God.

1st SUNDAY IN LENT

Jesus Tempted by the Devil

IN the desert Jesus fasted for forty days and forty nights. He was hungry. The devil tempted Jesus by asking Him to change stones into bread. Jesus refused. Then the devil promised to give Jesus riches if He would adore him, but Jesus would not do this or anything else that was wrong. So the devil went away.

When the devil tries to make you do what is wrong, pray to Jesus who will understand and help you.

On the Mountain

PETER, James and John climbed a tall mountain with Jesus. There they saw Him as they had never seen Him before. His face shone as the sun. His clothes were white as snow.

A voice from heaven said: "This is My beloved Son; hear Him." The apostles were afraid. Jesus touched them and told them not to fear. When they climbed down the mountain, Jesus told them not to tell anyone what they had seen until after He had risen from the dead.

3rd SUNDAY IN LENT

The Mother of God

OUR Lord went about doing good. He cast out devils. He worked many miracles. He cured the sick. He helped the poor. Wicked men tried to trap Him with questions, but He always gave perfect answers.

Good men and women loved Him. One woman praised His Mother. Jesus remembered how Mary had welcomed the angel who told her she was to be the Mother of God. He said that all who obey God are to be praised.

Five Loaves and Two Fishes

THE more miracles Jesus worked the larger grew the crowds. They liked to listen to Him talk, and they did not want to leave Him. One day Jesus told the apostles to give the crowd something to eat.

The apostles were worried because there were no stores and there were more than 5,000 hungry people. A little boy had a basket with five loaves and two fishes. Jesus blessed this food and there was more than enough for everyone.

PASSION SUNDAY

The Wicked Men

JESUS went about doing good for three years. He preached, He worked miracles, He told the people about their Father in heaven. Many Jews believed in Him. Some bad men asked Him many questions and tried to harm Him, but Jesus was never afraid.

One day they picked up stones to throw at Jesus, but He hid Himself and went out of the Temple. Jesus wanted all men to know, love and serve God, and be happy forever.

PALM SUNDAY

A Day of Victory

ONE beautiful spring morning Jesus rode into Jerusalem on a donkey. Along the road men and women, boys and girls spread their cloaks on the ground for Him to ride over. They cut palm branches to wave as He rode by. They shouted the same words that the priest says every day at Mass: "Blessed is He who comes in the name of the Lord!"

His Mother was glad that these people loved her Son. She is glad when we tell Jesus that we love Him.

The Lord Is Risen

EARLY in the morning Mary Magdalene carried spices to the tomb to anoint the body of Jesus. She was very much surprised to find an angel in the tomb. He told her not to be afraid, but to go back to Jerusalem and tell Peter and the other apostles that Jesus had risen from the dead, and that He would see them again.

Many times Jesus had told the people that He would die and that He would rise from the dead. All that He told them was true.

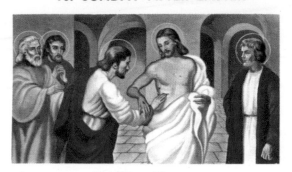

Doubting Thomas

WHEN Jesus appeared to the apostles on Easter Day, Thomas, one of the twelve, was not with them. When he joined them, they told him how they had talked with the Lord and eaten with Him. Thomas refused to believe. He said: "Unless I see the marks of the nails and put my hand in His wounds, I will not believe."

A week later Jesus appeared again to the apostles. He called Thomas and told him to touch His wounds. Thomas touched them and said: "My Lord and my God!"

2nd SUNDAY AFTER EASTER

Jesus is the Good Shepherd

A GOOD shepherd loves his sheep. He takes care of the little lambs. He gives them cool water to drink and leads them to green pastures. When the wolf comes, he is not afraid. He would rather die than let anything happen to his sheep.

Jesus loves all men. So He said that He is our shepherd. He will always help us. He comes to us in Holy Communion to make us strong. When we pray to Jesus, no harm can come to us.

Last Lessons

JESUS taught His disciples many lessons during the weeks between His Resurrection and His Ascension. He told them that He must return to God, His Father. He knew that this news would make them sad, but He wanted their sorrow to turn into joy.

Sometimes Jesus asks us to do something for Him that costs us very much and we are sad. But when we remember that He will be pleased, we ought to be happy. The happiness that Jesus gives us will last forever.

Jesus Promises to Send the Holy Ghost

FOR forty days after Jesus rose from the dead He talked to the apostles. He taught them many things. He told them that He would soon leave them. This news made them sad because they loved Him and wanted Him to stay with them.

He told them that after He had gone He would send them the Holy Ghost who would teach them to be strong and patient and truthful. We must ask the Holy Ghost to help us to be good.

5th SUNDAY AFTER EASTER

God the Father and Our Lord's Ascension

WHEN Jesus was living on earth, He often spoke to the disciples about His Father, and about His Ascension. He loves His Father, and He wants all men to know that His Father is powerful and good. The Father loves Jesus and sent Him into the world to teach men how to pray and how to serve the Father.

Whenever we say the *Our Father*, we are saying a prayer that Jesus taught the disciples. We must always say the prayer slowly and lovingly.

ASCENSION DAY

Jesus Ascends Into Heaven

WHEN Jesus rose from the dead, all those who loved Him were happy. For forty days they talked to Him and He visited them at meal time or at their work.

Then He told them that He had to leave them, and that they must believe in Him and tell others about Him. He blessed them and went up to heaven. While they were looking up into the sky, two angels told them to go back to the city and wait and pray.

In the Cenacle

AFTER our Lord ascended into heaven, the disciples went back to Jerusalem. They remembered that He had told them that He would send them the Holy Ghost who would make them brave and strong.

So they waited in the Cenacle which was the same room in which they had eaten the Last Supper. Our Lady was with them. They talked of many things that our Lord had told them, and for ten days they prayed.

The Holy Ghost

ON Pentecost Sunday the disciples were with our Lady in the Cenacle. Suddenly they heard a sound from heaven like the noise of a great wind. They saw tongues of fire, and they were filled with the Holy Ghost. They began to praise God, and to tell all the people how good God is and how wonderful are all His works.

The disciples understood, better than ever before, that God loves us and that we must do everything we can to show Him that we love Him.

TRINITY SUNDAY

The Blessed Trinity

THE mystery of the Blessed Trinity is found in the four Gospels. Saint Matthew, Saint Mark, Saint Luke and Saint John tell us many things about God the Father, God the Son, and God the Holy Ghost.

We honor the Blessed Trinity when we make the sign of the cross with love. We honor the Blessed Trinity when we say the Creed: "I believe in God the Father almighty . . . and in Jesus Christ, His only Son, our Lord . . . I believe in the Holy Ghost."

FEAST OF CORPUS CHRISTI

The Blessed Sacrament

ONCE when the crowds that followed Jesus were very happy, Jesus took the loaves and fishes that a little boy gave Him and fed thousands of people. The next day He told the people that He would give them the bread of eternal life. This bread is Holy Communion.

Jesus Himself comes to us in Holy Communion. Look at the Sacred Host and tell Jesus that you believe He is truly present, that you love Him and want to serve Him better.

The Great Supper

JESUS told many stories. One day He told the people about a man who invited his friends to a big supper. The friends made many excuses and said they could not accept the invitation. The man was very angry, and he sent his servants into the streets to bring in the poor, the blind, and the lame.

In this way Jesus taught the lesson that God loves all men, and that the poor and the sick are especially welcome in the kingdom of heaven.

FEAST OF THE SACRED HEART

The Sacred Heart

SAINT John stood beside our Lady when Jesus was dying on the cross. The disciple watched a soldier take a long sharp dagger and press it into our Lord's Heart.

John knew how much our Lord loves everyone, and he knew that our Lord wants everyone to love Him in return. He has given you many proofs of His love: He has given you a home and many kind friends. What can you give Him to show Him that you love Him?

Finding the Lost Sheep

EVERYONE is loved by Jesus, who wants all men to be good. Whenever anyone goes away and does what is wrong, Jesus is very sad. He said He is like a shepherd who has a hundred sheep. If one sheep is lost, the shepherd goes at once to look for it, and is happy when he has found it.

In heaven, too, all the angels rejoice when a sinner is sorry for his sins, and tells God that he loves Him.

The Miraculous Catch of Fish

JESUS loved to talk to the people about God the Father. He spoke to them in the city, on the mountains, in the desert, and on the seashore.

One day He preached to them from a boat. After the sermon Jesus told Peter to row out to the middle of the lake to fish. Peter obeyed at once, although he had fished all night and caught nothing. Jesus blessed Peter, and he caught so many fish that his boat began to sink.

Kindness to Everyone

IF WE want to please Jesus, we must be kind to everyone we know. That is what Jesus wants us to do at all times.

He told the disciples that they must never say an unkind word about anyone, never do an unkind thing to anyone, never even think an unkind thought. Whenever we forget what Jesus wants and we hurt anyone, we must tell him at once that we are sorry, then God will be pleased and He will hear our prayers.

The Miracle in the Desert

FOR three days Jesus talked to the people who loved to listen to Him. He told them about His Father, and how to please Him.

They were in a desert place and there was not enough to eat. Jesus felt sorry for them, so He asked them to give Him all the loaves of bread that they had. They brought Him only seven loaves. He blessed the loaves, and the disciples discovered that by a miracle there was enough food for 4,000 people.

Good Deeds Please God

TO please God we must do what God tells us. This was a lesson Jesus often taught His disciples. He showed them a fig tree, and told them that a good fig tree always gives good figs. He showed them a vine, and He told them that it will give good grapes and not thorns.

So you see that good children should always do good deeds, and some day God will come and take them to heaven where they will always be happy.

The Wicked Steward

JESUS wanted to teach His disciples that they must always be honest and make good friends, so He told them about the wicked steward.

This steward was about to lose his job with a rich man, and he did not want to beg or do hard work. So he turned to his friends who owed money to his master. He made them tear up their old contracts and write new ones with false amounts. By helping them to steal, he made sure they would help him later on.

The Cleansing of the Temple

THE marble Temple in Jerusalem was one of the most beautiful buildings in the world. When Jesus entered this holy place, He found merchants selling doves and lambs, money-changers seated at tables with gold and silver coins. This should never happen in the house of God.

Jesus made a whip of cords and drove the buyers and sellers from the Temple, saying: " 'My house is a house of prayer,' but you have made it a den of thieves."

The Pharisee and the Publican

IT IS wrong to boast. Jesus taught this lesson in this story. Two men went up to the Temple to pray. One was a Pharisee and the other a publican. The Pharisee went up to the altar and boasted that he was better than other men. He told of all the good things he had done.

The publican stayed near the door; he remembered how good God had been to him, and all he could say was: "O God, be merciful to me a sinner." God liked this prayer.

The Deaf and Dumb Man

A MAN who could not hear or speak came to Jesus to be cured. Jesus put His fingers in the man's ears, then He touched the man's tongue and said: "Be opened." At once the man could hear everything that was said, and he could speak clearly to Jesus and his friends.

All who watched Jesus cure this man were surprised, and they said: "He has done all things well; He has made both the deaf to hear and the dumb to speak."

The Good Samaritan

A LAWYER once asked Jesus, who was his neighbor. Jesus answered by telling this story. A certain man went from Jerusalem to Jericho. Robbers took away all his money and left him half dead.

A priest, a Levite and a Samaritan came along, but only the Samaritan stopped. He washed his wounds, took him to an inn and left money for his care. The lawyer understood that everyone was his neighbor and the Samaritan was a good neighbor.

Jesus Cures the Ten Lepers

ON the road to Jerusalem ten lepers waited for Jesus. Because they were sick, they had to keep away from other people, so when they saw Jesus they cried in a loud voice: "Jesus, Master, have mercy on us."

Jesus told them to go to the priest. On the way, they were cured. Only one of them returned to thank Jesus. Jesus blessed the grateful man. He was very sorry that the other nine men did not also give glory to God.

The Goodness of God

JESUS wants all men to know how good God is. He told His disciples to look at the birds of the air who do not sow, or reap, or gather into barns, but God gives them their food. He pointed to the lilies of the field which are more beautiful than the greatest king in his royal robes.

If we remember this lesson we will thank God for our home, our clothing, our food, because He has given us these things. God loves us and He shows us His love in wonderful ways.

The Widow's Son

WHEN Jesus came to the town of Naim with His disciples, they met a funeral procession. The people were sad because it was the funeral of the only son of a widow.

Seeing the mother's sorrow, Jesus was moved with pity. He told her not to cry, then He said to the dead young man: "I say to you, arise." And he who was dead sat up and began to speak, and Jesus gave him to his mother. Everyone in Naim rejoiced and praised God.

The Wedding Feast

JESUS knew that we tend to be selfish, wanting the best things for ourselves, so He taught us a lesson.

He said that when a man is invited to a wedding, he should not take the first place, because someone may come to him and tell him to take the last place. But if he chooses the last place, then he may hear the words: "Friend, go up higher." For everyone who exalts himself shall be humbled, and he who humbles himself shall be exalted.

The Greatest Commandment

A LEARNED man tried to test Jesus, so he asked Him this question: "Master, which is the greatest commandment in the Law?" Jesus said to him: "You shall love the Lord your God with your whole heart. This is the greatest and the first commandment. And the second is like it: You shall love your neighbor as yourself."

Jesus answered the people's questions so well, that after that day no one dared to ask Him any more.

18th SUNDAY AFTER PENTECOST

The Cure of the Paralytic

JESUS crossed over the lake and came into His own town. Some men brought Him a man who was lying on a pallet or a low bed. The man was not able to move.

Jesus saw the faith of those who carried the sick man, and so He said to the paralytic: "Take courage, son, your sins are forgiven you." Then to show that He could forgive sins, He said to the man: "Arise, take up your pallet and go to your house." And the man arose. He was completely cured.

The Prince's Wedding Feast

THIS story is about a king who made a wedding feast for his son. The first guests who were invited would not come, so the king punished them, and ordered his servants to invite good and bad men.

The king went in to see the guests and he saw a man who was not dressed properly. He told the servants to cast him outside. We must remember that if our souls are not filled with sanctifying grace, we cannot enter heaven.

The Sick Boy

THE son of a royal official was sick. When his father heard that Jesus was near, he went to Him and begged Him to come to his home and heal his child who was about to die. Jesus said: "Unless you see miracles you do not believe." But the officer begged more earnestly, saying: "Lord, come to my home before my little boy dies."

As soon as our Lord said to the sad father: "Go to your home, your son lives," servants came to say the boy was cured at that very moment.

FEAST OF CHRIST THE KING

Jesus Our King

EVERY time you look at a crucifix you can see that Jesus is a King. This is what the four letters— I N R I—mean in Latin. Pilate, the weak Roman governor, asked Jesus: "Are You a King?" Jesus told him that He was a King and that His Kingdom is a Kingdom of truth and love, of holiness and peace.

If we want to have Christ for our King we must try to please Him always. Let us pray that all men will belong to His Kingdom.

The Cruel Servant

IF WE love Jesus, we must forgive everyone who hurts us. Jesus taught this lesson in a story.

A servant owed a king some money but the man was too poor to pay his debt, so the king forgave him his debt. Then the servant met a friend who owed him some money, but the friend could not pay. The friend asked the servant to be merciful, but the servant refused and sent him to prison. When the king heard this he was angry, and punished the cruel servant.

22nd SUNDAY AFTER PENTECOST

Cæsar's Coin

THE Pharisees wanted to take Jesus prisoner, so they sent two spies to ask Him if it was good to pay taxes to the Romans.

Jesus asked them to show Him a big silver coin. He held it in His hand and said: "Whose image and whose name are these?" They answered: "Cæsar's." Jesus gave them back the coin, saying: "Render to Cæsar the things that are Cæsar's, and to God the things that are God's."

The Daughter of Jairus

WHEN the boat bringing Jesus across the lake reached shore, a man named Jairus was waiting. He knelt before Jesus and said: "My daughter is dying; come lay Your hand on her that she may live." Jesus then followed him to his home.

There all were crying; they said the little girl was dead. But Jesus went in and, taking her hand, said: "Maid, arise." The girl stood up and began to walk.

24th AND LAST SUNDAY AFTER PENTECOST

The Last Judgment

OUR real home is in heaven. Some day this world will come to an end. The sun will be dark. The moon will give no light. The stars will fall from the sky. God will come upon the clouds with great beauty and power. He will send His angels to blow their trumpets.

Then the good will be happy with God forever in heaven. The wicked will be punished in hell. We must love God and help others to love Him, so that we will all be with God.

Dec. 8—IMMACULATE CONCEPTION

Our Immaculate Mother Mary

ONE day when Mary was praying in her home, an angel suddenly stood before her. It was the angel Gabriel, who said: "Hail, full of grace, the Lord is with you; blessed are you among women."

Mary was the most beautiful, the most wise, and the most pure of all God's creatures. She never did anything that was wrong; her soul was never soiled by sin. For this reason God the Father loved her and chose her to be the Mother of Jesus.

The Faithful and Obedient St. Joseph

SAINT Joseph was the head of the Holy Family. He worked as a carpenter to support Jesus and Mary. He was a man of prayer as well as a man of work.

God sent angels to tell Saint Joseph all that he needed to know. An angel told him that Jesus was the Son of God. Another time when Herod wanted to kill Jesus, an angel appeared to him and told him to take Jesus and Mary into Egypt. Saint Joseph obeyed at once.

August 15—THE ASSUMPTION OF THE BLESSED VIRGIN MARY

The Magnificat

OUR Blessed Mother is our model. She was kind to everyone. She visited her cousin Elizabeth and made her very happy. When Elizabeth heard Mary's voice, she cried out: "Blessed are you among women, and blessed is the fruit of your womb."

Mary replied in a beautiful prayer of praise that many people still say today: "My soul magnifies the Lord and my spirit rejoices in God my Savior." Our Lady is now happy in heaven. She will help us to love God.

Nov. 1—FEAST OF ALL SAINTS

The Communion of Saints

TODAY the Church reminds us of the saints in heaven. They praise God with the angels. They honor our Lady the Queen of Angels.

Some day we will be in heaven, if we obey the lessons our Lord preached in the Sermon on the Mount. He said that to be happy we must be poor in spirit; we must be meek; we must sorrow for our sins; we must try to be holy; we must be merciful; we must be pure; we must be peaceful, and willing to suffer for God.

The Living Bread

G OD made us to know, love, and serve Him in this world, so that we can be happy forever with Him in the next. After we have lived on earth as long as God wills, He will come and take us to heaven.

To help us to live as He wishes, He gives us His Body and His Blood in Holy Communion. He said: "He who eats My Flesh and drinks My Blood has life everlasting."

The souls in purgatory need our help. Pray for them often.

Vestments and Objects for Mass

ALTAR STONE   CHALICE AND PATEN   CRUCIFIX   AMICE   ALB

CHALICE VEIL AND BURSE   MISSAL   ALTAR CARDS   CINCTURE   STOLE

PALL FOR CHALICE   CORPORAL AND PURIFICATOR FOR CHALICE   BELL   MANIPLE   CHASUBLE

Vestment Colors

WHITE—means joy and purity.
RED—means suffering for God's love.
GREEN—means hope in God.
PURPLE—means sorrow for sin.
BLACK—means sadness.

DAILY PRAYERS

The Our Father

OUR Father, who art in heaven, hallowed be Thy name; Thy kingdom come; Thy will be done on earth as it is in heaven. Give us this day our daily bread; and forgive us our trespasses, as we forgive those who trespass against us; and lead us not into temptation, but deliver us from evil. Amen.

The Hail Mary

HAIL Mary, full of grace! the Lord is with thee; blessed art thou among women, and blessed is the fruit of thy womb, Jesus. Holy Mary, Mother of God, pray for us sinners, now and at the hour of our death. Amen.

The Glory Be

GLORY be to the Father, and to the Son, and to the Holy Ghost. As it was in the beginning, is now, and ever shall be, world without end. Amen.

The Apostles' Creed

I BELIEVE in God, the Father Almighty, Creator of heaven and earth; and in Jesus Christ, His only Son, our Lord; who was conceived by the Holy Ghost, born of the Virgin Mary, suffered under Pontius Pilate, was crucified, died, and was buried. He descended into hell, the third day He arose again from the dead; He ascended into heaven, sitteth at the right hand of God the Father Almighty; from thence He shall come to judge the living and the dead.

I believe in the Holy Ghost, the holy Catholic Church, the Communion of Saints, the forgiveness of sins, the resurrection of the body, and life everlasting. Amen.

Act of Faith

O MY God, I believe in You, and I believe all that the Holy Catholic Church teaches.

Act of Hope

O MY God, I hope in You; please forgive my sins and lead me to heaven.

Act of Love

O MY God, I love You with all my heart and soul because You are so great and so good.

Act of Contrition

See page 123.

Grace before Meals

BLESS us, O Lord, and these Your gifts, which we are about to receive from Your bounty, through Christ our Lord. Amen.

Grace after Meals

WE thank You, O God, for these gifts and for all the gifts we have received from Your goodness, through Christ our Lord. Amen.

Morning Prayers

O MY God, I believe in You, I hope in You. I love You above all things. I thank You for having brought me safely through this night.

I give my whole self to You. Everything I do today, I will do to please You. Keep me, dear Jesus, from all evil. Bless my father and mother, and all those I love.

Holy Mary, pray for me.

Our Father. Hail Mary.

Evening Prayers

O GOD, I thank You for the many blessings I have received today. Forgive me all my sins. I am sorry for them all because I have displeased You. Bless me while I sleep so that I may do better tomorrow. Bless my father and mother and all those I love, and make them happy.

Jesus, Mary and Joseph, help me, especially in the hour of my death. Amen.

Our Father. Hail Mary.

PRAYERS FOR CONFESSION

I Must Think of My Sins

I will try to find out my sins by asking myself these questions:

How many weeks has it been since my last confession?

Have I missed Mass on Sundays and Holy Days?   Have I been late for Mass?

Have I laughed or talked in Church?

Have I missed morning and night prayers?

Have I disobeyed my parents or teachers?

Have I gone with bad children?

Have I looked at bad pictures?

Have I told lies?

Have I stolen anything?

Have I said bad words?

Have I eaten meat on Friday?

Have I been angry?

Be sure to tell the Priest HOW MANY TIMES you have committed a sin.

An Act of Contrition

O MY God, I am heartily sorry for having offended You and I detest all my sins, because of Your just punishments, but most of all because they offend You, my God, who are all-good and deserving of all my love.

I firmly resolve, with the help of Your grace, to sin no more and to avoid the near occasions of sin. Amen.

AFTER CONFESSION

Say the penance the priest gave you.

JESUS, You have taken away all my sins. With this pure soul of mine I wish to live for You alone, only to obey You, only to please You. I am happy now because my soul is at peace.

JESUS, I thank You for taking my sins away. Help me to keep my soul free from sin. May I never hurt You again.

DEAR Mother Mary and my Guardian Angel, always keep me close to Jesus.

Say the Our Father and the Hail Mary.

PRAYERS FOR HOLY COMMUNION

BEFORE HOLY COMMUNION

SWEET Jesus, with this Holy Communion, I offer You today, my thoughts, my words, and all that I do. May Your grace help me to be always ready to receive You.

An Act of Faith

O GOOD Jesus, You are now on the altar. I believe that You are the same God who made heaven and earth, and who became a child like me to draw us all close to You. I believe that now You are really present in Holy Communion to be the food of our souls. I believe it all because You said so.

An Act of Hope

O GOOD Jesus, You come to me with the riches of heaven and earth. I truly hope that You will bring me all the help I need to serve You well and to get to heaven.

An Act of Love

DEAR Jesus, how much I should love You, after all that You have suffered for me! Make me grow more and more in love for You. How happy I shall be when in a few moments I shall hold You close to my heart.

An Act of Contrition

I KNOW, dear Jesus, I have often offended You by my sins. But I am very sorry now. One word from Your holy lips, and my soul will be whiter than snow. I promise, dear Jesus, to be very careful not to offend You again.

An Act of Adoration

MY LORD and my God, I believe that You are really present in the Blessed Sacrament. I adore You, O Jesus, my Creator, my Lord, my Redeemer, my Love.

Come, dear Jesus, come into my heart. I am going to receive You in Holy Communion. You are God.

My Lord and my God!

AFTER HOLY COMMUNION

Prayer to Thank Jesus for Coming to Me

SWEET Jesus, Your miracles are very great. Your greatest miracle is that of giving Your Body and Blood to us in Holy Communion. This is You Yourself and not just bread.

I thank You for giving Yourself to me. May this Holy Communion bring me closer to You, my Lord and my God.

Acts of Faith, Hope, Love and Petition

O GOOD Jesus, You are King of heaven and earth. I believe in You. I hope in You. I love You.

Please bless my father and mother and all my family. Bless the priests, who have done so much for me; also bless my teachers and my friends.

An Act of Joy

MAY my soul always want You, O sweet Jesus.

May You always be with us in Holy Communion.

May You live in my heart always.

May Your many graces help me to be happy with You forever in heaven.

An Act of Offering

O JESUS, You have given Yourself to me; now let me give myself to You. I give You my body, that it may be chaste and pure. I give You my soul, that it may be free from sin. I give You my heart, that it may always love You. I give You every thought, word and deed of my life, and I offer all for Your honor and glory.

Jesus, for You I live; Jesus, for You I die; I wish to be Yours forever.

Say Prayer Before a Crucifix inside front cover.

THE STATIONS OF THE CROSS

THE Stations of the Cross remind us of the many things Jesus suffered in order to save us from sin. They help us to understand how much He loved us. When we make the Stations of the Cross, it is like following Jesus from one place to the other and seeing what He suffered.

HOW TO MAKE THE STATIONS

Before each Station, genuflect and say:

"We adore You, O Christ, and we bless You; because by Your Holy Cross, You have redeemed the world."

Then think about the scene before you, for a few moments. The short prayers under each Station may be helpful. After the last Station, say one Our Father and Hail Mary for the Pope.

1. Jesus is Condemned to Death
Dear Jesus, help me to sin no more and to be very obedient.

2. Jesus Bears His Cross
Dear Jesus, let me suffer for sinners in union with You.

129

3. Jesus Falls the First Time
Dear Jesus, help those who sin
to rise and to be truly sorry.

4. Jesus Meets His Mother
Dear Jesus, may Your Mother
console me and all who are sad.

5. Jesus is Helped by Simon
Dear Jesus, may I do all things
to please You all day long.

6. Veronica Wipes His Face
Dear Jesus, give me courage
and generosity to help others.

130

7. Jesus Falls a Second Time
Dear Jesus, teach us to be
sorry for all our many sins.

8. Jesus Speaks to the Women
Dear Jesus, comfort those who
have no one to comfort them.

9. Jesus Falls a Third Time
Dear Jesus, show me how to be
obedient and to be very kind.

10. He is Stripped of His Garments
Dear Jesus, teach me to be
pure in thought, word and deed.

131

11. Jesus is Nailed to the Cross
Dear Jesus, keep me close to You from this moment until I die.

12. Jesus Dies on the Cross
Dear Jesus, be with me when I die and take me to heaven.

13. He is Taken from the Cross
Dear Jesus, teach me to place all my trust in Your holy Love.

14. He is Laid in the Tomb
Dear Jesus, help me to keep the commandments You have given.

THE HOLY ROSARY

THE Rosary calls to mind the most important events in the lives of Jesus and Mary. These events are called Mysteries and are divided into the following 3 groups:

The JOYFUL MYSTERIES help us to think of Mary's joy when Jesus came into the world.

The SORROWFUL MYSTERIES help us to think of Mary's great sorrow when Jesus suffered for our salvation.

The GLORIOUS MYSTERIES help us to think of the glorious Resurrection of Jesus and the Crowning of Mary as Queen of Heaven.

HOW TO SAY THE ROSARY

1. Say the Apostles' Creed.
2. Say 1 Our Father.
3. Say 3 Hail Marys.
4. Say 1 Glory Be, then announce the 1st Mystery and say 1 Our Father.
5. Say 10 Hail Marys and 1 Glory Be.
6. Announce 2nd Mystery and continue in the same way until each of the 5 Mysteries is said.

1. The Annunciation to Mary
Mary, Jesus will be your Son.
Teach me to love Him.

The Five

Joyful

Mysteries

2. The Visitation
Mary, you visit your cousin
Elizabeth. Help me to be kind.

4. The Presentation
Jesus, You are offered to God
in the temple. Help me to obey.

3. The Birth of Jesus
Jesus, You are born in a stable.
May I value grace above money.

5. The Finding in the Temple
Jesus, You are found with the
teachers. Give me true wisdom.

134

The Five Sorrowful Mysteries

3. The Crowning with Thorns
Jesus, You receive a crown of thorns. Give me true courage.

1. The Agony in the Garden
Jesus, You are saddened by my sins. Give me true sorrow.

4. The Carrying of the Cross
Jesus, You carry the Cross gladly. Help me to be patient.

2. The Scourging at the Pillar
Jesus, You are whipped by the soldiers. Help me to be pure.

5. The Crucifixion
Jesus, You die on the Cross for me. Keep me in Your grace.

1. The Resurrection
Jesus, You rise from Your tomb.
Help me to believe in You.

The Five

Glorious

Mysteries

2. The Ascension
Jesus, You go to Your Father in
Heaven. Help me to hope in You.

4. The Assumption of Mary
Mary, You are taken to heaven.
Let me be devoted to you.

3. Descent of the Holy Ghost
Holy Ghost, You come to bring
grace. Help me to love God.

5. The Crowning of Mary
Mary, You are crowned Queen
of Heaven. Let me serve you.

136

"The Lord be with You" Jesus Appears to the Apostles.

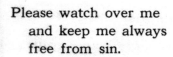

Prayer to the Holy Family

JESUS, Mary and Joseph,
   I give you my heart
and my soul.

Please watch over me
   and keep me always
   free from sin.

Bless my family,
   my friends and teachers,
   and all Priests and Sisters.

Grant peace to all people
   on earth and lead us
   to you in heaven.